MW00949075

Loose

Tooth

Written and Illustrated

by

Adina R. Travis

Copyright © 2017 Adina Travis

All rights reserved.

ISBN: 978-1542732956
ISBN-13: 1542732956

DEDICATION

This book is dedicated to my loves Qasim, Bria, and Naraya

Q came running into the kitchen on a Saturday Morning shouting, "Mom look!"

Q stood up straight and proudly opened up his mouth. "I can wiggle my tooth with my finger."

Q's mother turned away from the kitchen sink where she washing dishes, she could tell Q was very excited.

"Let me see it Q." She took the tip of her finger and put it on the tip of his tooth. Sure enough, it was wiggly.

"Oh, you have your first loose tooth."

Q was feeling a little curious about what was going to happen next.

"Mom what does that mean?"

Mom walked back towards the kitchen sink to finish washing the dishes.

"It means it's going to come out, and a new one will grow in its place."

Q cut his eyes to the side, then he walked over and placed his two hands on the edge of the counter so that he was directly in his mother's elbow space, then he asked,

"Why mom?"

Q's mother lifted her arm then looked down at him, wondering why he needed to be in her elbow room to ask that question. Then she replied,

"Because your baby teeth have to come out so that your adult teeth can grow in."

Q looked down at the floor while he contemplated the thought. Then he grabbed his mother's arm and asked,

"Like you mom?"

Q had regained her undivided attention again. She looked at him and replied.

"Yes Q"

"Ok then." Q replied and then walked out of the kitchen.

Q sat on the floor in his bedroom wondering about what it would be like to have adult teeth.

I wonder what I will look like when I get my adult teeth. I wonder if I can do whatever I want like adults do when I get them.

The next morning Q comes in the kitchen for breakfast. He walks over and sits down at the table in front of the bowl of cereal that had been waiting for him for about 15 minutes.

Hey mom!

Q's mother was sitting at the table having tea, Breeze and Ray sitting on both sides of her. Q sat down in the chair right across from her. She looked up from her tea.

"Good morning Q." Then she notices his tooth is missing.

"Q what happened, did your tooth fall out?"
"Yes, it fell out." Q says without even looking up from his cereal.

Q's mother gets up out of her chair and walks around the table to him to get a better look,

"Well, where is the tooth?" "Where did you put it?" she asked.

Q continued to eat his cereal. He responded in a nonchalant tone.

"I don't know".

Q's mother stood next to him with her hand on her hip.

"What do you mean you don't know?"

Q slid out of his chair and carried his bowl over to the sink, without even turning around, then he replied;

"Mom, I don't know."

He begins to walk out of the kitchen.
Mom stops him before he hits the doorway.

"Q, when your teeth fall out; bring them to me.

Q is beginning to think maybe this is an even
bigger deal than he thought.
He looks up at his mother and asks,

"Why?"

"Because", I will keep them," She replied.

"Why?" Q asked.

"Because," "I can make a keepsake."
Q then asked, "What is a keepsake?"

"A keepsake is something of value that you save.
It helps you to remember something important."
His mother replied.

Q cut his eyes to the side as he contemplated the thought of a keepsake. Then his face lit up, and he asked

"Like pictures mom?"

She looked at Q and smiled feeling proud of his intelligence, and then she replied.

"Yes like pictures."

"Ok then" Q replied, and then walked out of the kitchen.

Later that day, Q visits his dad and his grandmother. The girls decided to stay with mom for the day.

Q's father was sitting outside on the front steps. Q hops out of the car and runs up to the house.

"Hey Dad"!

"Hey Q," What's up man?"

He noticed that Q was missing a tooth so he kneeled down to get a better look.

"Hey, I see you lost your first tooth."

Q's face lit up. "Yeah dad, I was just about to show you."

"Where is your tooth Q?"

Q begins to walk away and responds without even turning around.

"I don't know".

"What do you mean you don't know?" Q's father asked him.

Q continues to walk away as he replies in his nonchalant voice,

"Dad I don't know."

Dad stands up and follows Q toward the house. "Well when your teeth fall out, bring them to me."

23

Q stopped walking, then turned around and walked right into his dad.

Q backs up a few steps, then he asks,

"Why dad?" "Cause you want a keepsake?"

"No," "because I will give you money". Dad replied.

"Here is 5 dollars." "Next time bring me the tooth."

Excited about his 5 dollars, Q runs into the house to say hello to his grandmother.

"Hey Grand mom"!

Q's grandmother stood up to prepare for the embrace.

"Hey baby. I missed you" she said as she gave Q a big squeeze.

"I missed you too Grand mom."

Then she notices that Q lost a tooth. For fun she decided to act like she didn't notice. "Q there is something different about you but I just can't put my finger on it."

Q got real excited. "Grand mom I… "No wait don't tell me, she interrupted".

She puts her finger across her chin, and looks down at Q.
 "I know…you got taller"
Nope, that's not it, Q replied.

"You got a new haircut."
"Nope wrong again"

Q opened up his mouth and pointed to the space in his mouth.

"See, I lost a tooth, he said with his mouth still wide open.

"Oh Yes I see now, that's awesome Q."
"Did you get a visit from the tooth fairy?"
Q raised his eyebrow in wonder. "The tooth fairy… Who is that?"

Q's grandmother couldn't help but laugh. Then she explained.

"When your tooth falls out, you put it under your pillow. Then the tooth fairy comes to get the tooth from under your pillow while you are sleeping."

"Why," "because she wants a keepsake?"
"No," "Because she will leave you a quarter for your tooth."
"Well I already got 5 dollars from my dad for the tooth and I didn't even have the tooth."

"Oh well I guess you got a better deal then."
"Yup," Q replied.

"Ok go run and play then"

As Q sat and played with his toys, he wondered why grown-ups make such a big fuss about baby teeth.

Adult teeth are way more important than baby teeth. Then he thought about who he should give his next tooth to.

Mom wants a keepsake. Dad will give me money, and the tooth fairy will visit me while I am sleeping and leave me a quarter.

One week later Q ran into his mother's bedroom with excitement.

"Hey mom look". He shouted.
"I lost another tooth."

Mom sat up on the edge of the chair.
"Well where is it Q?"

"I don't know."

"What do you mean you don't know Q?"

"Mom I don't know

Made in the USA
Monee, IL
04 September 2022

13222157R00024